THE KINGDOM WAY OF LIFE
Restoring What It Means to Follow Jesus

PARTICIPANT'S GUIDE

—

Q Group Studies

Five Sessions

GABE LYONS AND NORTON HERBST

ZONDERVAN®

ZONDERVAN.com/
AUTHORTRACKER
follow your favorite authors

ZONDERVAN

Q Study: Kingdom Way of Life Participant's Guide
Copyright © 2011 by Q

Requests for information should be addressed to:
Zondervan, Grand Rapids, Michigan 49530

ISBN 978-0-310-67137-4

Published in association with Yates & Yates, www.yates2.com.

Printed in the United States of America

11 12 13 14 15 16 /DCI/ 32 31 30 29 28 27 26 25 24 23 22 21 20 19 18 17 16 15 14 13 12 11 10 9 8 7 6 5 4 3 2 1

TABLE OF CONTENTS

The Kingdom Way of Life 1

Welcome to Q Studies 4

Your Place in Culture 6

Group Gathering One: Did Jesus Preach the Gospel? 9

Q Short: Living the Gospel in Culture 27

Group Gathering Two: Living the Kingdom in Culture 45

Group Gathering Three: The Both/And of the Gospel...59

Group Gathering Four: The Transformative Kingdom 77

Culture-Shaping Project: Learning While Doing 94

Group Gathering Five: Seeking the Hidden Treasure 97

—

THE KINGDOM WAY OF LIFE: RESTORING WHAT IT MEANS TO FOLLOW JESUS

Jesus began his public ministry with these words: "The time has come. The kingdom of God has come near. Repent and believe the good news!" (Mark 1:15) Not long after that, he said to Peter and Andrew, those blue-collar fishermen, "Come, follow me, and I will send you out to fish for people" (Mark 1:17). So, for the first disciples, the invitation to follow Jesus was an invitation to the kingdom of God. And 2,000 years later, the same invitation remains for us today.

So, what does it mean to truly follow Jesus? What do we believe about this good news, or gospel, of the kingdom of God? Few of us today understand this concept of kingdom very well. We live in democratic societies where elected officials come and go according to the will of the people. We no longer answer to the fiat of a king.

On one hand, that's a good thing. Hardly anyone in the West would argue that a democratic form of human government is inferior to the often-repressive monarchies of past history. On the other hand, we find it hard to comprehend our role in God's kingdom where the totality of our lives is ordered by the "kingship" of Jesus. In this Q Study, your group will explore what it means to follow Jesus and accept his gospel message, not just in our minds and heart, but also in our very lives—to embrace the kingdom way of life.

THE KINGDOM WAY OF LIFE

WELCOME

WELCOME TO Q STUDIES

Q Studies are designed to convene small groups of people to dialogue, learn, and work together to help you navigate the tensions of following Jesus in a post-Christian culture. Q Studies are actually based on an old idea—the Society Rooms of the late 1600s. These small gatherings of leaders that would convene, dialogue, learn, and work together to strengthen their faith and renew their culture. Consider the impact of these early Society Rooms:

In 1673 Dr. Anthony Horneck, a Church of England minister in London, preached a number of what he called "awakening sermons." As a result several young men began to meet together weekly in order to build up one another in the Christian faith. They gathered in small groups at certain fixed locations and their places of meeting became known as Society Rooms. In these gatherings they read the Bible, studied religious books and prayed; they also went out among the poor to relieve want at their own expense and to show kindness to all. By 1730 nearly one hundred of these Societies existed in London, and others—perhaps another hundred—were to be found in cities and towns throughout England. The Societies movement became, in many senses, the cradle of the Revival … (Arnold Dallimore, *George Whitefield*, Vol 1., Crossway, 1990, pp. 28–29)

Following this historical example, this Q Study is designed to renew your minds as leaders so that you can live out your faith and make a difference in society. As you begin meeting together, your group should be characterized by a commitment to put learning into action. And no doubt, over the course of the next few weeks, your innermost beliefs and preconceived ideas about life, faith, the world, and your cultural responsibility will be challenged. But that's the point.

Here's how it works. Your group will gather five times to discuss important topics related to the overall theme of this study. Sometimes you'll be given something to do or read before your group gathers. It's important for you to take these "assignments" seriously. They won't demand much time, but they will require intentionality. Doing these things ahead of time will cultivate a richer and more stimulating group experience as you begin to practice what you are learning.

For each group gathering, set aside about one hour and fifteen minutes for the discussion in a place with minimal distractions. Your group may want to share a meal together first, but be sure to allow enough time for unhurried dialogue to take place. Sometimes you'll watch a short video. But conversation and dialogue will always be the priority. The leader of the group will not teach or lecture, but instead will ask questions, facilitate conversation, and seek input from everyone. Be prepared to ask good questions and share your own thoughts. Sometimes you'll even debate an issue by taking sides and thinking through all the complexities. The goal of each gathering is for your group to be stimulated by a particular idea and learn together as you discuss its impact on your faith, your lives, and culture in general. Your group may not arrive at a consensus regarding any given topic. That's okay. Be respectful of others, even when you disagree with them. We can learn something from everyone.

Before your fifth gathering, you will undertake a group project together. You may be tempted to skip this. Don't! Your group project might be the most important part of your experience. Genuine learning as a community takes place when you *engage* the ideas you are discussing and *do* something together as a group.

In the end, be committed to this group and the learning process that is about to ensue. Your willingness to prepare for group gatherings, keep an open mind, and demonstrate eagerness to learn together will pave the way for a great experience.

YOUR PLACE IN CULTURE

INTRODUCTIONS

At the beginning of your first gathering, spend about fifteen minutes introducing yourselves to one another and discussing your channel of cultural influence.

There are several different social institutions that touch every person in a given society. These areas of influence contain most of the industries and organizations that consistently shape our culture. They touch every aspect of our lives, and most of us find our vocational roles in one or more of these areas. They are the seven channels of cultural influence.

As you begin your Q Study experience, you'll notice that most, if not all, of these channels are represented in your group. Start your first gathering by sharing which particular channel of influence you participate in. Give the rest of the group a sense of how your channel contributes to shaping society in general. Then, throughout the rest of the group experience, reflect on how your learning will affect the channel to which you've been called.

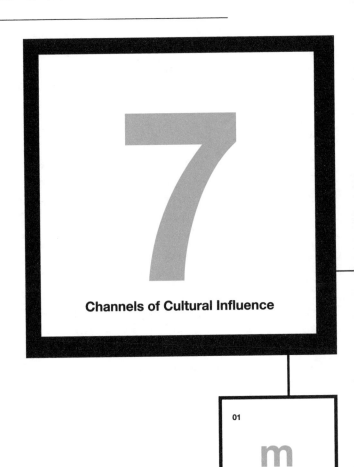

7

Channels of Cultural Influence

01

m

media

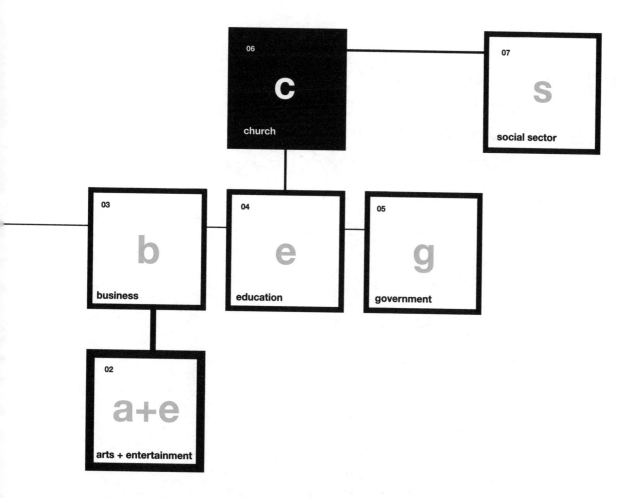

If you believe what you like in the gospels, and reject what you don't like, it is not the gospel you believe, but yourself.

AUGUSTINE

The gospel to me is simply irresistible.

BLAISE PASCAL

The only significance of life consists in helping to establish the kingdom of God; and this can be done only by means of the acknowledgment and profession of the truth by each one of us.

LEO TOLSTOY

DID JESUS PREACH THE GOSPEL?

IT STARTS WITH THE GOSPEL

Spend a few minutes sharing your thoughts with the group.

Everything about the Christian faith—the beliefs, practices, and institutions that embody following Jesus—begins with the defining message of the gospel. So, what exactly do we mean when we use this term "gospel"? What do you associate with this word? How has it been used in our culture?

DISCUSSION STARTERS

When were you first exposed to this term "gospel"? How did someone (a friend, parent, teacher, pastor, or priest) explain it to you?

Have you ever seen a "gospel tract"? How do these short booklets often describe the gospel?

Can you define the gospel in one sentence? If so, how? If not, why not?

ORIGINS OF THE TERM "GOSPEL"

The Greek word that is translated "gospel" in the New Testament is *euangelion*. In classical Greek literature, it had two primary meanings:

(a) A message that brought joy to its hearers, often about a military or political victory.
(b) News about an imperial emperor's birth, coming of age, enthronement, speech, decree, or act that brought long hoped-for fulfillment of peace and prosperity in the world and that established the ruler's divine origins. For example, note an inscription from 9 BC (a few years before Christ) marking the birthday of Caesar Augustus:

It is a day which we may justly count as equivalent to the beginning of everything—if not in itself and its own nature, at any rate in the benefit it brings—inasmuch as it has restored the shape of everything that was failing and turning into misfortune, and has given a new look to the Universe.... Whereas the Providence which has ordered the whole of life, showing concern and zeal, has ordained the most perfect consummation for human life by giving to it Augustus, by filling him with virtue for doing the work of a benefactor among men, and by sending in him, as it were, a saviour for us and those who come after us, to make war to cease, to create order everywhere.... The birthday of the God [Augustus] was the beginning for the world of the glad tidings [Greek euangel] that have come to men through him.

Source: Ulrich Becker, "Gospel" in New International Dictionary of New Testament Theology, *Colin Brown, gen. ed., vol. 2, pp. 107-108.*

DID JESUS PREACH THE GOSPEL?

WATCH

View Q Talk: Did Jesus Preach the Gospel? by Scot McKnight.

Record your thoughts on the talk on page 15.

Scot McKnight is a widely recognized authority on the New Testament, early Christianity, and the historical Jesus. He is the Karl A. Olsson Professor in Religious Studies at North Park University (Chicago) and the author of more than twenty books, including the award-winning *The Jesus Creed*.

The term "gospel" is often misused. Some define it so broadly that it has lost its meaning. Others define it narrowly according to the apostle Paul's writings about "justification by faith." All this leads New Testament scholar Scot McKnight to ask: did Jesus himself preach the gospel? At Q Chicago, Scot explained what is and what isn't the gospel message.

—

"When the gospel means everything, it loses all meaning."

—

"We have developed a personal salvation culture at the expense of a gospel culture."

—

"The gospel is the announcement, the declaration, the heralding that Jesus is Messiah, Redeemer, and Lord. He lived and he died and he was buried and he rose again and he is coming again. As the raised and ascended One he is Lord of both Jews and Gentiles and that is the gospel of the New Testament."

—

"No one in the New Testament calls the plan of salvation the gospel."

THOUGHTS

—

AN ACADEMIC DEBATE?

—

Split the group into two sides and spend fifteen minutes debating the issue:

Is this discussion about defining the gospel just an academic debate that doesn't make a big difference in everyday life?

Even if you don't agree with the side you are representing, consider and offer the best arguments for your position. Be respectful.

Record your thoughts on pages 18-19.

Use the following debate starters to guide your time.

Scot McKnight explains four approaches to the concept of "the gospel":

- The whole story of the Bible from beginning to end.

- The specific announcement of Jesus as Messiah and Lord.

- The plan of salvation: putting your faith in Jesus and experiencing justification.

- The method of persuasion: convincing others about their need to trust Jesus.

He proposes that it's vital for Christians to explore these approaches and come to the conclusion that the gospel is first and foremost an announcement about who Jesus is. And as a New Testament scholar who is passionate about interpreting the Bible correctly, it's easy to see why he thinks this is so important.

But, is this discussion about defining the gospel just an academic debate that doesn't make a big difference in everyday life?

DEBATE STARTERS

Christians believe that understanding the gospel message is vital for salvation, but how important is it when it comes to the stuff of our everyday lives—going to work, raising kids, paying the bills, etc.?

Is there really a big difference between understanding the gospel as an announcement versus equating it with God's plan of salvation for people? What are implications of each viewpoint?

In order to understand the gospel message, is it more important to look at Jesus' teaching and actions or the writings of later New Testament authors like Paul? Why?

—

YES

This discussion about defining the gospel is just an academic debate that doesn't make a big difference in everyday life.

THOUGHTS

_

NO

It's essential for Christians to define the gospel accurately—everything else we believe and do flows from that.

THOUGHTS

—

THE KINGDOM OF GOD

—

Have a few people in your group take turns reading this section aloud.

What was the most dominant theme in Jesus' teaching? Heaven and hell? No. Reading the Bible? Prayer? No. Serving the poor? Well, he did talk about that a lot, and you could say it was a big concern of his. But there was one theme that took center stage in his teaching, one idea he talked about more than anything else: the kingdom of heaven, or the kingdom of God. Why? Because it had so much to do with who he was and the mission he had for his followers.

At its heart, the expression "kingdom of God" simply refers to God's rule on earth through Jesus as the King. That's why the gospel—the announcement that Jesus is Messiah, Lord, and King—is so central to the concept. But, as followers of Jesus, there are enormous implications for us.

Scot McKnight explains it well in his book, *The Jesus Creed* (Brewster, Mass.: Paraclete Press, 2004, pp. 126-127):

> What does [Jesus] mean by "kingdom"? Ask a Christian "What did Jesus mean by 'kingdom'?" and you will get something like this: "heaven, eternity, life after death." Or you might hear: "heaven on earth, the millennium, a perfect world,

paradise." (On my unscientific questionnaire, the responses are about fifty-fifty.)

"Kingdom of God" is Jesus' favorite expression for his mission. The gospel of Matthew sums up the entire ministry of Jesus like this:

> *Jesus went throughout Galilee, teaching in their synagogues, preaching the good news of the kingdom, and healing every disease and sickness among the people.*

So, if "kingdom of God" is so important to Jesus, what does it mean? I offer this thumbnail definition: *the kingdom is the society in which* the Jesus Creed [loving God, loving others] *transforms life.*

Thus, the kingdom of God is not just about God's rule in our world through Jesus. It's also about our role as subjects and ambassadors of the kingdom by which we bring transformation to our lives and *our* world.

REFLECTION STARTERS

Spend a few minutes journaling your thoughts to the two questions below. Then, share your reflections with the group.

How often do you think about your way of life—your daily habits, actions, and routines—as living out the kingdom of God in this world?

What does it mean to pray that part of the Lord's Prayer that says: "your kingdom come, your will be done, on earth as it is in heaven" (Matt. 6:10)?

JOURNAL

JOURNAL

—

WE ARE ANNOUNCERS

ACT

—

The Christian life begins with an understanding of two concepts: gospel and kingdom. Everything about our faith starts with our response to the announcement that Jesus is the Messiah and Lord and through him, God's rule has broken into our world and our lives. And in that response, we ourselves become announcers of the gospel and the kingdom.

What specific areas of your life have you not surrendered to Jesus' kingship and rule?

—

LIVING THE GOSPEL IN CULTURE

PREPARE FOR NEXT GATHERING

—

Before your next gathering, read the Q Short Interview with Michael Metzger beginning on page 28. Be sure to set aside some uninterrupted time for this. Try not to save it until the last minute. When you read the essay, underline, highlight, or jot down comments about ideas (on page 43) that are particularly interesting, disconcerting, or challenging. Be prepared to share why at the next gathering.

Q SHORT

LIVING THE GOSPEL IN CULTURE

LIVING THE GOSPEL IN CULTURE
Gabe Lyons interviews Michael Metzger

Gabe: *Let's start from the beginning with this idea of "worldview." You have a unique way of describing what a worldview is and where it shows up in our own lives and in the lives of others. Could you share that with us?*

Mike: Well, I have a few ways, actually. Two young fish are swimming along and they happen to meet an older fish swimming the other way. He nods at them and asks, "Morning, boys, how's the water?" The two young fish swim on for a bit. Eventually one of them asks the other, "What the hell is water?"

Worldview is water passing through our gills. Or it's the eyeglasses an individual wears. One criterion for a great pair of eyeglasses is *comfort*. I've enjoyed excellent vision all of my life. But when I turned 47, my wife Kathy noticed I was rubbing my eyes in the morning while reading the paper. "Why don't you buy some reading glasses?" *What*, I replied, *and* spend hundreds of dollars on eye exams and glasses? "You knucklehead, they cost about ten bucks and require no exam!" So I purchased a pair and could now see the paper more clearly ... but I've never become comfortable with eyeglasses draped across my nose. I'm uncomfortably *aware* of them. In most cases, "worldview" constitutes *what we are unaware of*. It's our unconscious assumptions, not our conscious beliefs.

Here's how worldviews work: When I was a little kid, I snuck into my parents' bedroom one afternoon (as though it was off limits!) and looked in Dad's closet. I noticed the shoes were in a neat row on the floor while the shirts and jackets were categorized by colors. But I cannot recall hearing my dad saying, "Ve are German and everything vill run on time and you vill line up your clothes very neatly by sizes and colors." It was just an unconscious assumption that *this* is the way a closet ought to be.

That's what we mean by "worldview." A few words of caution: few people outside Christian circles talk about or use the word "worldview." We have to be careful about too much group speak or using ghetto language. We also need to exercise caution in how we speak of "changing a worldview." People often talk about shifting paradigms. This language comes from Thomas Kuhn in his book *The Structure of Scientific Revolutions*. We get giddy about going off to a weekend conference and then come back proclaiming to have made six or seven paradigm shifts. We fail to recognize that Kuhn said very few people make paradigm shifts, since they include repudiation of old paradigms, repentance from them, and changing assumptions.

Kuhn was right; a worldview is tough to see, tougher to acknowledge, and toughest to change. It's like describing air to a bird and water to a fish. It's all we know and we assume it's all that's ever been. Fish in the filthy Anacostia River assume dirty water *is all there is*. "Clean water" is merely a concept, without meaning. The fact is, fish only become aware of the water they swim in when they are *removed* from the water. Do fish find this experience to be enjoyable? Hardly, it feels more like death.

This is why few make paradigm shifts. A real one feels like death. Assumptions that we assume are sacred are hard to topple. For example, one very deep assumption in Western Christianity is the Enlightenment's idea of human, scientific rationality—that the core of our being is our cranium. The Hebrew mind, on the other hand, believed we think with our bodies and know by doing. If those in the modern Western church embraced the Hebrew model, most of the ways we preach, teach, and mentor would be toppled. That would imperil the careers of those who publish this stuff. Better to keep the machine running. I run the risk of redundancy when I say this, but worldviews or paradigms are hard to change. They might throw you out of work.

Another way to understand worldview is to picture it as your diet. Technically, a diet is anything you eat; so you don't "go on a diet." You either have a good, better, or bad diet. In the same way, you don't "go find a worldview" or "get a worldview." In fact, it's really hard even to "cultivate a worldview." It *can* be done, but worldview is simply the way you see the world without thinking much about it. It's been shaped by school, friends, geography, ethnicity, background, gender, institutions, images, items

WHERE IN THE BIBLE DID GOD SAY,"NAIL JOHN 3:16. DON'T SWEAT 3:13."? HE DOESN'T. WE SIMPLY ASSUME JOHN 3:16 IS PARAMOUNT.

... a zillion things. Findings from neuroscience indicate we can only be consciously aware of around 5 percent of these influences.

Gabe: *So, is there a "Christian worldview"?*

Mike: No, there isn't a "Christian" worldview. Someone, probably C. S. Lewis, observed that "Christian" is not an adjective in the Bible. So, there really isn't a "Christian" worldview. The biggest problem with this label is that you can't honestly critique anything that's "Christian." Music, books, churches, films, anything that gets the "Christian" label becomes a "no-fly zone" that can't be critiqued (because it's "Christian").

There can be what we call "biblically faithful worldviews" that try to conform to what the Scriptures say. The problem is that every epoch in history gets it right in some areas and doesn't get it right in others. For instance, there were those who believed they had a pretty cultivated worldview on what constitutes a human being. The reality is that their definition didn't include black people. They would've, however, been mortified if you had suggested that their worldview wasn't "Christian." They just could not imagine at the time that they were wrong.

This is reality for everyone, including me. In my line of work, I apply myself to the 80-20 rule: 80 percent of what I'm saying is close to the truth (including this interview) while 20 percent is not. The problem is I don't know what part constitutes that 20 percent at this moment. It would take an uncomfortable experience— someone suggesting some of my assumptions are incorrect—in order for me to say, "Ah, I never thought about that." Who enjoys that?

We all live and have our being inside a set of unspoken assumptions. For example, I'll often ask a religious group: "Quote for me John 3:13." Usually, the silence is deafening. Then I'll say, "You know, that's interesting. Where in the Bible did God say, 'Nail John 3:16. Don't sweat 3:13.'? He doesn't. We simply assume John 3:16 is paramount." I call John 3:16 the Evangelical Empire State Building. It blots out the sun for many blocks in every direction. Within our worldviews, certain verses mean more than others. This is not entirely bad. Nor do the differences necessarily indicate a deficiency in anyone. It just simply means we read Scripture with a set of eyeglasses. The best eyeglasses are the most comfortable ones—the ones we're unaware of. *That's* worldview. And worldview precedes even the Bible.

One of the more striking examples of worldview shaping data can be seen in the work of the late Harvard scientist Stephen Jay Gould. He was a good friend of Carl Sagan and others in that ilk. They all started with one basic assumption or worldview. "There is no God—now let's go do science!" But what Gould was never willing to concede is that his view, just like a Christian's, begins with a set of faith assumptions. They may be right, they may be wrong, but you can't prove or disprove them, including existence of God, one way or another. You can't scientifically or theologically prove there is a God and you can't prove there isn't. It's a faith assumption. That's what we mean by worldview. These assumptions lurk below the waterline.

Gabe: *In today's culture, is it safe to assume that worldviews might be largely shaped by postmodernism versus modernism? How much do the values of the wider culture around us shape our worldview?*

Mike: It is difficult to become self-aware. I'm not a skeptic, but there are very few Christians that I meet who say, "I'm willing to be pulled from my warm body of familiar water and wiggle on the end of a line in a thoroughly different environment." It feels like abandonment and disloyalty to the gospel. Yet without this kind of occasional introspection, it's exceedingly hard to discover how much I've been shaped by New York, Madison Avenue, L.A., Seattle, or Berkeley. And it's an especially hard task for Christians. We get what I call the "God Glaze." Once I embrace Christ and meet God, then I tend to simply assume that what I hold to is

biblically based. But that's not necessarily true. So we have a myriad of influences shaping our assumptions, along with the sense of responsibility that we're to be faithful to God.

You mentioned postmodernism versus modernism. That in itself is a dichotomy largely derived from modernism, or the Enlightenment. Hegelian Idealism—the assumption that *ideas shape worldviews more than institutions*—largely shaped the German Enlightenment. Postmodernism and modernism are *ideas*. But in reality, it is images and icons and institutions that more profoundly shape worldview. Thus, the very question of worldviews being largely shaped by postmodernism or modernism is misguided. See how discovering our unconscious worldviews is unsettling?

In an ironic sort of way, most of my friends who have not embraced Jesus are more open to having assumptions challenged. They don't suffer the "God Glaze." Christians ought to feel the weight of truth that would make us more pliable, not more puffed up or rigid. Discovering our assumptions *will* produce "cognitive dissonance." The man who coined that term, Leon Festinger, found that religious people are more prone to cognitive *resistance* when they have their worldviews challenged. It's ironic yet a sad statement about the state of faith today.

Another way to think about our assumptions is to imagine a Christian from the fourth century joining our dialogue today. They might hear the language you use and the way you describe Christianity and ask, "What are you talking about?" And you'd say, "I'm talking about Christianity. What are you talking about?" And they'd say, "That's not the Christianity we embraced." Did you notice the difference? The majority of ancient hymns and prayers were in the plural "we" or "our" while most today are in the first-person singular—"I."

We are shaped by far more than the Bible, our friends, God, and our church—even though these are pretty significant. The piety that is not particularly healthy among some Christians is this assumption that they are unscathed by culture when, in fact, it's ubiquitous. We are all shaped by culture. It's far, far more than ideas. It's institutions and images.

Gabe: *Does our culture even shape our understanding of the gospel?*

Mike: Absolutely. In my work, we often talk about the gospel as being grounded in "four chapters" that you'd find in any good story. Chapter one is the *Creation*, chapter two is the *Fall*, chapter three is *Redemption*, and chapter four is *Restoration*, the consummation of history. These four chapters are found in the Apostles'

Creed, the Nicene Creed, the Athanasian Creed, the Heidelberg Catechism, all the way up to the sixteenth and seventeenth centuries.

When we take a look at history, what we call "evangelical" is fairly recent. We all agree that "evangelical" means "good news." And of course, the good news goes back all the way to the beginning of Scripture. But no one called themselves "evangelical" until Luther's followers. Then after the Diet of Speyer they were called Reformers. So "evangelical" went out of use with the exception of a few of the English Puritans. The term "evangelical" came back into use when the original reformed groups were in dire need of reform. A new kind of "evangelical" came into existence. This group included Finney and they formed the Second Great Awakening. Evangelicals were what I call "turbochargers." They forced more air and life into the existing engine blocks of Methodists, Baptists, Congregationalists, and the like.

This is the biggest "brand" of evangelicals today, if you like. They got going in the early and mid-1800s and focused more on the inner life, giving it more juice—just like a turbocharger. Revving the engine block meant thinking less about creation and culture. In fact, since we assumed everyone understood the "four-chapter" grounding of the gospel, evangelicals focused on the specific two chapters of *Fall* and *Redemption*. "Come forward," "Walk with Jesus," "Share your faith with other people," and "Pray to receive Christ" became the common coinage of these new evangelicals. This led to the development of an unprecedented and unbiblical "two-chapter" gospel—what Nancy Pearcy calls a *truncated* gospel. The *Creation* and final *Restoration*, which included redeeming the entire world, fell by the wayside. Dallas Willard calls these truncated messages gospels of *sin-management*. Their message will indeed get you to heaven, and they have spawned a few religious revivals. But the problem with a turbocharger is that it's not an engine. It doesn't provide horsepower, it amps up the existing power. And that would eventually spell trouble.

When the great engine blocks of Lutheranism or Congregationalism or Methodism fell into disrepair, we evangelicals were stuck sucking air. When these historical institutions began to fade, evangelical turbochargers were no longer anchored in great traditional theologies (or engine blocks). Evangelicals became the anti-institution religion, focusing almost solely on the inner life. The "two-chapter" gospel eclipsed the historic "four chapter" good news.

Gabe: *So, if you understand the gospel as situated in light of all four chapters, your life reflects different values and you engage the world differently. Another way of thinking about it is what you describe by using four terms: ought, is, can, and will be. Would you unpack those concepts for us?*

Mike: I'm drawn to writers like C. S. Lewis and Peter Berger, a sociologist at Boston University. These men would say that there are patterns and pointers in our experience and in the universe. If you can find these patterns, they point to something beyond. If you can tease out common experiences we all share in, you can—by trial and error—begin to hear and see these patterns. You don't have to start with the Bible. The most common pattern I've discovered—and it fits everyone everywhere—is that we all imagine our life in terms of how it *ought* to be, *is*, *can*, or *will be*. It's a cosmic code. And it's ground in creation.

We think about life the way it *ought* to be because of *Creation*. There is design. We recognize our life as it is because of the *Fall*; there is a default. We think about what we *can* do to make life better because of *Redemption*. And finally, we dream about what *will* be because we're made for eternity, the final *Restoration*. That's our destiny. This universal pattern can only be explained by the gospel. The Eastern family of faiths can't explain it. Darwin or Nietzsche can't explain it.

In my own experience, the more I became immersed in this "four-chapter" grounding of the gospel, the more it explained the warp and woof of life. It accounts for transportation and eating and food and work and recreation. Think of stuff—like quiet times, home groups, church, and reading. Those are critical, but they don't account for enough of our day. If the gospel can't explain

HUMAN BEINGS CAN PROCESS UNCONSCIOUSLY PERHAPS 14 MILLION BITS OF INFORMATION PER SECOND.

it this way: track the 168 hours in your week and write down everything you do—for example, we work 55 hours a week, sleep 56, commute for 10, eat, prepare food, clean up, take showers, talk to friends, watch TV and spend time on the Internet, etc. In my conversations with Christians, most of them cannot connect the good news to their work, play, leisure, recreation, workout regimen, what they eat, sleep patterns, daily commute, and viewing habits. How is the gospel connected to Blackberries? If you can't answer that question with some level of coherence and clarity, then most folks are left with a few minutes or an hour or two when they can do all their "spiritual"

all the things we do all day—that is, the way they ought to be, the way they are, what you can do about them, and what they will be—then you have a gospel that can get you into the kingdom but will have trouble with "Thy kingdom come."

Gabe: *What does it mean for us to pray: "Thy kingdom come"? How should that shape the way we live our lives?*

Mike: First, this is the only place in Scripture where we are "allowed," so to say, to command God. The verb is in the imperative—"Lord, I want your kingdom to come ... now!" We should live with an expectation that we are privileged to partner with God in having dominion over and making culture in our world. This, of course, assumes that faith communities put the horse before the cart.

By that, I mean putting the Cultural Mandate before the Great Commission. The Cultural Mandate appears in Genesis 1:26–28 where God calls Adam and Eve to reign and reproduce. This project begins in the Garden, where Adam is told to "cultivate" the earth (Gen. 2:15). "Cultivate" is translated in German as *kultur* and where we get our word "culture." It's our "human job description," writes Dallas Willard. We are to *make culture.* Even after Adam and Eve fell, the Cultural Mandate is restated in Genesis 3:23 ("cultivate the ground") and after the flood in Genesis 9. It has never been rescinded and was historically considered to be the horse that pulls the cart.

The Great Commission calls the church to *make disciples.* However, in some American faith communities, *this* is the horse. The Cultural Mandate tags along as the cart—something the church commits resources to only *after* winning people to Christ and trying to disciple them. But if these churches aim to develop "fully devoted followers of Christ," their view of the horse and cart is undermined by neuroscience findings indicating how the human brain operates.

Human beings can process unconsciously perhaps 14 million bits of information per second, according to John Gray of the London School of Economics. The bandwidth of what we're conscious of, however, is only about 18 bits. The rest of human behavior is unconscious, or culturally conditioned—about 99.99999 percent. Yet, in reality, we know the brain does not process data in "bits" in the computing sense. Our brains have well-developed filtering and compress the information. This is why the percentage of *bundled* images we unconsciously process is not 99.99999. Rather, it's closer to 95 percent according to Cal Berkeley professor George Lakoff. It's still a lot.

The implication from this research is that faith communities *can't* make "fully devoted" *Christians* without first making a *culture* fully devoted to a biblical definition of reality. They have to put the horse—the Cultural Mandate—before the cart, since behavior is more culturally conditioned than a matter of choice—by a wide margin. *This* is the chief way that "Thy kingdom come"—in alignment with the Cultural Mandate—should shape our lives.

Gabe: *So followers of Christ are to help bring God's kingdom into our world. But we also understand our role as being "in the world but not of it." So how should Christians respond when they feel like they are in the middle of a culture that seems so corrupt and decadent?*

Mike: A couple of things come to mind. First, it *is* a society that is corrupt and decadent. Second, in the best sense of the word, not enough Christians are in the "middle of a culture." I think it was Os Guinness who said we have enough Christians in society but they are not the right kind of Christians. If you are mixing it up with real live people in real live situations in the wider world, you're going to get enmeshed in some pretty cruddy stuff, or sin. Historically, Christians have understood that there was a difference between sin that provoked us and sin that offended us. It's not a real clean divide because your level of response has a lot to do with the health of your conscience. Remember, conscience is what God gave us that he didn't give the animals; it demarcates us from the animals. It's our moral compass speaking to us about right and wrong. Here's the paradigm: the healthier the conscience, the more that evil and sin in the world provokes us (rather than offends us). In the Scriptures, being provoked always leads to engagement. And that's the kingdom way of life.

Think about when Paul, for example, went to Athens. It was a highly pornographic city, yet he spent the whole day studying its sullied culture. Kind of like flying to Amsterdam and walking up and down the red-light district really taking it all in. Yet the sin of Athens provoked Paul. Most Christians flee such a scene. And I can hardly blame them! Yet our ability to withstand such an onslaught of sin is directly proportional to the health and strength of our conscience. If we pull the lens back, we see Jesus Christ who enjoyed an eternally wonderful existence in heaven that was as far away from sin as it could be. What was it like for him to arrive in Bethlehem? Wasn't it a pretty yucky world he dove into? Why didn't he get a whiff of sin—having never tasted it—and hightail it to the hills? Or why didn't he start a commune in Iowa just to get away from the big bad world? Because he was *provoked* by sin. The sin of the world caused Christ to roll up his sleeves and say, "We have to do something about it."

Now that's one side of the coin regarding our response to sin. On the other side, the weaker your conscience, the more the sin actually offends you instead of provoking. And offense leads to withdrawal. Don't misunderstand—all sin is bad. But when you're provoked, as Moses was with the golden calf, you roll up your sleeves and go after it. When you're offended, you run for the hills. Sometimes it's good to run for the hills. When Potiphar's wife was hitting on Joseph, Joseph headed for the hills. Her sin was offensive, and it ought to have been offensive. That was a good move.

Obviously there's no hard and fast rule here. It has a great deal to do with the health and strength of your conscience. That's why alcoholics and rehabilitating drug addicts are very offended when other people drink around them and they can't get near the door of a bar; they have probably defiled their conscience to a great degree. That's sad but understandable, in some regard. The challenge is not mandating that for everyone else. People who are offended very easily tend to mandate for other people what is appropriate for them and what isn't.

Gabe: *How can someone work on having a healthy conscience?*

Mike: So few people have even written on it anymore. I would say to do all that you can do to pick up on the thirty-one times in the New Testament that the conscience is mentioned. Start with Paul who said, "I've lived my whole life with a clear conscience." He was smart, but it didn't mean that he got everything right. I would say a person with a healthy conscience is someone who has a lot of emotional intelligence, that is to say—they are self-aware. If you want to get serious about having a healthy conscience, I would get three or four friends that will be completely honest and have them ask you, "What are you unaware of?" Compare notes. See who is closer to reality. In the Old Testament, prophets performed this service. In King Arthur's court, they are called court jesters. In the Mafia, it was a consigliere. In recent literature shaped by this view of human nature, they are called satirists. Ernest Hemingway called them crap detectors. Either way, see if it hurts so much when they cut it straight with you that you

shut down. If so, you probably don't have a very healthy conscience. If you say, "You know there are some things that I'm not aware of. I really want to become self-aware"—and then truly take in what you hear, you're probably moving toward being a person of a healthy conscience. And you're becoming more useful for the kingdom.

Gabe: *It seems like being part of a strong community of faith is vital for engaging culture in this kind of engaging way. What does a kingdom-minded community look like?*

Mike: I was with a group last Friday morning and one of our friends had recently returned from Africa. He was saying, "What can I do about the challenges of Africa?" I responded, "Listen, don't worry about Africa for the moment. Here's a question: Do you think more people ought to take mass transit?" And he said, "Yeah." I said, "Great. You figure out what it would take to get 10 percent of *our local village* to take mass transit. Once you figure that out, then you'll figure out what needs to be done in Africa." He immediately began to see the layers and layers of institutions and individuals needed to pull it off. City councils, automakers, rail lines, funding, etc.

So, what would community be? Let me be frank with you for a moment. One of the deepest problems in the modern Western church is this Enlightenment view of human nature. Its mantra is: "Education is the answer." In the church, this assumption is that Christians just aren't smart enough, don't know enough Bible, and need to get into small groups to study more and gain a "Christian" worldview. I think that's wrong.

Community needs a cause. Community is a group of people tackling a *real-life problem* in the wider world. Period. Community is not a Christian *cult-de-sac* studying "biblical principles of work," for example. This is why the entire cottage industry of "truth projects" and "worldview seminars" is misguided in my opinion. They are static, packing truth as principles that need to be applied. I hate to be the bearer of bad news, but the Bible never uses "application" in this sense. Rather, it speaks of individuals *applying themselves* to real-life problems and learning about reality as they get dirt under their fingernails. Adam applied himself to Eve, and off they went to Knowledge Land. It's why sex outside of marriage was once considered carnal knowledge. You didn't get that from seminars! Think about community in terms of a fellowship and how Tolkien framed up fellowship. Fellowship was a task—throwing the ring in the mountain of Mordor.

Community, if you look at what any decent sociologist says, is merely yada yada until it becomes a habit. And therein lies our problem. Community is *not* a habit of American life. We

are pretty naïve about what Alexis de Toqueville noticed all the way back in the 1820s. He coined a new word to describe American culture: individualism. Today, individualism is institutionalized. Cars (instead of mass transit), most of the world's single-family homes, or Facebook (instead of sitting in groups with real, live people) characterize our life. In Switzerland, community is institutionalized. I can walk out of my hotel's front door at eight minutes past every hour and hop on a bus. From that point on, I'm connected to all of Europe via rail. In the U.S., you have to take a car to get to the rail that basically takes you to very few destinations.

If you want to talk about "developing a community," steal a page from the recycling industry. Recycling has become a habit in our family. It became a habit because *systems* were put in place all the way down to the yellow barrels. They are picked up every Tuesday. It is solving a real problem. I do my part. If you're going to change habits, like getting people out of cars into mass transit or getting them to recycle, take one area and work it out. You'll soon say, "Oh my goodness! This is going to take a lot of overlapping institutions and individuals."

When I think about real community, I'm drawn back to my time in sports. In playing sports, a couple of things are nonnegotiable. You *will* do what you're told to do. The huddle is not a Senate committee for discussion. You have a boss. You show up on time. You get in shape. You do what's required. You play to win. You overcome real obstacles. And, you may never be heard of. That's community.

Gabe: *So a kingdom-minded community that brings God's will to bear in our world is not just the people you might call friends or acquaintances or even neighbors. True community is created with the people that you work together with to sustain your life and calling.*

Mike: Habitat for Humanity does very well in this case, but it also shows why the "bottom up" approach to changing the world is often ineffective. In terms of community, I hear stories all the time of people who stay in touch with people they worked with to build a house. They see something tangible. But when you see what it takes to build one Habitat home—we're talking about 100–130 people, quite a bit of resources, hundreds of hours of time—it's not a realistic plan to make broad changes in the housing market.

If you want to change the housing industry, we need additional "top down" institutions and communities influencing national builders, lenders, developers, real estate sellers, etc. For all the good that Habitat has done, more people have lost their homes since 2008—or are upside down—than all the homes that have been built by Habitat since it began. My point is that we need both bottom up and top down.

This is why, when someone says they are going to raise up a whole generation of twentysomethings who are going to embody a Christian worldview, I say, "Shuwee! More power to ya!" I would encourage them to crunch it down to one locality, one church, one school, and say: "There … I'm working with one school right now." When you begin to work in a community, your grandiose statements come under the influence of gravity. That's good. It's easy to yak about this stuff. All we then become are talking heads. I think that James Hunter is right when he says that we have a culture of celebrity in this country—especially evangelicals—where a lot of us have become talking heads. But we don't have anywhere near enough teaching hospital models where someone could say, "Show me where that's actually working out."

Gabe: *So, Mike, you've been living out the gospel in culture for years. I know you've come alongside people like me in this journey of living the kingdom way of life. What advice would you give to others who want to embrace that mission?*

Mike: One way to start is just getting back in touch with this "four-chapter" grounding of the gospel. I would also urge anyone to go beyond *knowing* and start *doing*. I'd take a C-level leader out to lunch and ask him or her: "Tell me your five biggest challenges." See if you can assist them in solving any one of those problems.

In my opinion, this is how we learn what the Bible means. The Enlightenment said you can observe a text, you can interpret it, you can know the whole meaning and then you can go out and start to apply it. Adam would have never known the deepest meaning of sex without having experienced it with Eve. Bible knowledge goes well beyond book knowledge. *Doing* something as a step of faith always precedes discovery. You don't know something—truly know it—until you actually do it. It's like riding a bike. You can go to seminar after seminar about riding a bike, but the best thing to do is go out and ride a bike. Skin your knee.

This is a lesson I needed to learn back in 1995. That year I resigned as a pastor and went underground. I began to meet with people all over the place. What I found was that a lot of the stuff I was teaching was irrelevant to everyday life. If as a pastor I wanted applause, I was a hit. But if I was after discipleship and *meaning*, I had to go back and confront my paradigms chief of which was my Enlightenment assumption: I had always assumed that if I've taught it and you've heard it, I can now assume that you *know* it! Untrue. I had to

repudiate my old paradigms, repent of them, and change many assumptions.

Of course I'm not advocating for reckless activism nor am I against pastors and preaching. What I'm urging is that you start with this reality of a gospel centered on the person and work of Christ, yet stretching from one end of the universe to the other and explaining everything. Then go out and actually do "faith and work"—but start at the other end. Try doing "work ... and *then* faith."

Michael Metzger *is one of the best-kept secrets in the body of Christ today. He is the president of The Clapham Institute, whose mission is "to align organizations and people with an accurate assessment of human nature." TCI assists businesses and churches in a mentoring and consultant capacity. Mike is also the author of* Sequencing: Deciphering Your Company's DNA. *Recently, Gabe Lyons sat down with Mike to explore how our understanding of the gospel impacts the way we live our lives, and ultimately our influence on culture.*

JOURNAL

JOURNAL

History has brought us to the point where the Christian message is thought to be essentially concerned only with how to deal with sin … a gospel of sin management.

DALLAS WILLARD

I have been impressed with the urgency of doing. Knowing is not enough; we must apply. Being willing is not enough; we must do.

LEONARDO DA VINCI

Jesus was going around "doing the kingdom," healing the sick, cleansing lepers, feeding the hungry, he was celebrating at a party with all the wrong people, transforming people's lives and saying cryptic things such as: "Let me tell you what the kingdom of God is like."

N. T. WRIGHT

LIVING THE GOSPEL IN CULTURE

—

FOUR CHAPTERS TO THE STORY

DISCUSS

—

In the last gathering, Scot McKnight described how the gospel—the announcement of who Jesus is—is embedded in the whole narrative of the Bible. Michael Metzger explained this gospel narrative in four parts—Creation, Fall, Redemption, and Restoration. What are your thoughts about this way of framing the gospel message?

DISCUSSION STARTERS

Have you ever considered how Creation is a crucial part of the biblical story and gospel message? Why or why not? What happens if we leave it out?

Why is it so easy for Christians to focus on Fall and Redemption and lose sight of the first and last "chapters"?

How would you explain the difference between Redemption and Restoration?

What do we lose if we end the story at Redemption?

THE ROMAN ROAD TO SALVATION

A COMMON WAY TO "SHARE THE GOSPEL" IN THE TWENTIETH CENTURY WAS KNOWN AS THE ROMAN ROAD TO SALVATION. IT DESCRIBED THE GOSPEL USING FIVE WELL-KNOWN VERSES IN PAUL'S LETTER TO THE ROMANS. HOW DOES IT COMPARE TO THE FOUR-CHAPTER UNDERSTANDING?

CREATION ▢   **FALL** ▢   **REDEMPTION** ■   **RESTORATION** ▢

Romans 3:23: For all have sinned and fall short of the glory of God.

Romans 5:8: But God demonstrates his own love for us in this: While we were still sinners, Christ died for us.

Romans 6:23: For the wages of sin is death, but the gift of God is eternal life in Christ Jesus our Lord.

Romans 10:9: If you declare with your mouth, "Jesus is Lord," and believe in your heart that God raised him from the dead, you will be saved.

Romans 10:13: For, "Everyone who calls on the name of the Lord will be saved."

KNOWING AND DOING

Split the group into two sides and spend fifteen minutes debating the issue:

Is Metzger right—that it's more important to our faith and role in the world to focus on doing, or is he undervaluing the role of education in forming our beliefs first?

Even if you don't agree with the side you are representing, consider and offer the best arguments for your position. Be respectful.

Record your thoughts on pages 50–51.

Use the following debate starters to guide your time.

Michael Metzger made the bold claim that education is overrated in the church and "knowing" more often comes from doing rather than precedes it. He warns:

> In the church, this assumption is that Christians just aren't smart enough, don't know enough Bible, and need to get into small groups to study more and gain a "Christian" worldview. I think that's wrong.... The entire cottage industry of "truth projects" and "worldview seminars" is misguided in my opinion. They are static, packing truth as principles that need to be applied. I hate to be the bearer of bad news, but the Bible never uses "application" in this sense. Rather, it speaks of individuals *applying themselves* to real-life problems and learning about reality as they get dirt under their fingernails.

Is Metzger right—that it's more important to our faith and role in the world to focus on doing, or is he undervaluing the role of education in forming our beliefs first?

DEBATE STARTERS

Do you often conclude that the reason Christians aren't making a significant difference in the world is an education problem?

Does Christian community become more transformative when people are learning together or doing together?

Do you think the contemporary American church places too much emphasis on education or action?

Why is there often such a big disconnect between Christians knowing what is true and actually applying that truth in their lives?

—

YES

We've become too focused on education; it's more important to our faith and role in the world to prioritize doing.

THOUGHTS

—

NO

Our actions stem from our worldview—what we believe to be true. Actions will only change when people learn new beliefs and then apply them.

THOUGHTS

GETTING LOCAL

Have a few people in your group take turns reading this section aloud.

Michael Metzger emphasized the importance of bringing redemption and restoration in your local community first. He told a story:

> I was with a group last Friday morning and one of our friends had recently returned from Africa. He was saying, "What can I do about the challenges of Africa?" I responded, "Listen, don't worry about Africa for the moment. Here's a question: Do you think more people ought to take mass transit?" And he said, "Yeah." I said, "Great. You figure out what it would take to get 10 percent of *our local village* to take mass transit. Once you figure that out, then you'll figure out what needs to be done in Africa." He immediately began to see the layers and layers of institutions and individuals needed to pull it off. City councils, automakers, rail lines, funding, etc.

It's not that we can't contribute value to issues in other parts of the world. But God has given us gifts and responsibilities to demonstrate his kingdom values in our own communities. And often times, we can make a much greater difference locally. Aside from charitable giving, we're often ill-equipped to address issues in other parts of the world. While some are specifically called to that role, most of us will make the greatest kingdom impact in our own families, workplaces, schools, and neighborhoods. "Your kingdom come, your will be done, *in my neighborhood,* as it is in heaven."

REFLECTION STARTERS

Spend a few minutes journaling your thoughts to the two questions below. Then, share your reflections with the group.

In your own neighborhood, where do you see that God's kingdom has not come?

How can your lifestyle tangibly demonstrate kingdom values to others in your neighborhood?

JOURNAL

JOURNAL

LIVING THE KINGDOM

ACT

Living out the gospel means being a witness to God's kingdom in your life. It starts with the Cultural Mandate—creating culture that is *good* for society—and continues through the Great Commission—helping others to embrace the kingdom way of following Jesus. And it only happens in community.

Would you characterize your small group or church as a kingdom-minded community? If so, why? If not, what needs to change?

—

THE BOTH/AND OF THE GOSPEL

—

For the next week, spend fifteen minutes every morning praying through the Lord's Prayer in Matthew 6:9–13. After a few days, it may feel repetitive, but keep it up. When you come to the phrase "your kingdom come, your will be done, on earth as it is in heaven," reflect on the specific areas of your life where you want to see God's kingdom, or will, extend. Is it your attitude, your workplace, your relationships, or your dreams? Make your prayers specific to your life.

Spend the final portion of your time together discussing your culture-shaping project.

PREPARING FOR YOUR CULTURE-SHAPING PROJECT

In the next few weeks, your group will take part in a project together to apply what you are learning and discussing. It's important that you complete this project before your last gathering. Three options for what your group can do have been recommended on pages 94-95. All of them require some planning and preparation. Take a few minutes now to read the options and discuss which one best suits your group. You don't have to make a decision this week, but you need to get the ball rolling and be prepared to make a decision and start planning at your next group meeting.

A kingdom founded on injustice never lasts.

SENECA

There is no justification without sanctification,
no forgiveness without renewal of life, no real
faith from which the fruits of new obedience
do not grow.

MARTIN LUTHER

God is a God of both justice and justification.

JOHN STOTT

GROUP GATHERING THREE
THE BOTH/AND OF THE GOSPEL

OUR CONCEPT OF JUSTICE

DISCUSS

Spend a few minutes sharing your thoughts with the group.

Your group has discussed the concepts of gospel and kingdom. A related idea is justice (more on the connection shortly). When you hear the term "justice," what do you think of?

DISCUSSION STARTERS

What comes to mind when you hear the word "justice"?

How does justice take place in our current legal system?

How would you define the opposite term, "injustice"?

Are justice and injustice primarily legal concepts, or are there moral and spiritual dimensions?

HOW MUCH DO WE SPEND ON JUSTICE IN AMERICA?

Direct Expenditure by Criminal Justice Function, 1982–2006

BILLIONS

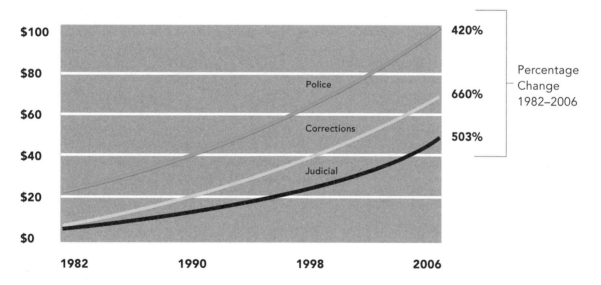

Percentage Change 1982–2006

Source: U.S. Department of Justice Bureau of Justice Statistics at http://bjs.ojp.usdoj.gov/content/glance/exptyp.cfm

—

THE BOTH/AND OF THE GOSPEL

—

View Q Talk: The Both/And of the Gospel by Tim Keller.

Record your thoughts on the talk on page 65.

Tim Keller is the senior pastor of Redeemer Presbyterian Church in Manhattan and author of the *New York Times* bestseller *The Reason for God*. Tim has led the PCA denomination's church planting initiatives and remains committed to promoting and nurturing the growth of new churches in New York City and around the world.

The twenty-first century church often polarizes itself into those who are socially involved in issues of justice and those who emphasize evangelism and doctrine. Both camps tend to believe that they are living out the kind of kingdom values that Jesus taught. But Tim Keller asserts that these two extremes present us with a false choice. At Q Chicago, he explained that the gospel presents us not with an either/or dichotomy, but a both/and mission.

—

"Other religious systems say, 'Live as you ought, and then God will accept and bless you.' But the gospel of justification by faith alone says, 'No, you can receive God's acceptance and blessing right now as a free gift because of what Jesus has done, and then, and only then, can you and will you live as you ought.'"

—

"Justification and justice are joined at the hip. They are almost a seamless cloth."

—

"Isaiah says, 'If you say you believe you're a sinner saved by grace, but you don't care about the poor, you haven't really encountered God's grace, you're not really right with God."

—

"To be a Christian, you've got to admit that you're spiritually bankrupt … you're poor in spirit and that means when you, the spiritually poor, meet the materially poor, you'll never be condescending again.… Anybody who understands the doctrine of justification by faith alone—you're looking at a mirror when you look at a poor person."

THOUGHTS

WHAT DOES THIS WORLD NEED?

DEBATE

Split the group into two sides and spend fifteen minutes debating the issue:

Is addressing issues of injustice the most important way we can influence our culture, or is it more important to tell people about Jesus and the spiritual salvation he offers?

Even if you don't agree with the side you are representing, consider and offer the best arguments for your position. Be respectful.

Record your thoughts on pages 68-69.

Use the following debate starters to guide your time.

Tim Keller presents a compelling argument. Those who have truly experienced God's grace (justification) become ambassadors of that grace in our world (justice). The two go hand in hand in the kingdom of God. Yet, a debate remains about which aspect of this kingdom way of life is most needed in our culture today.

Is addressing issues of injustice the most important way we can influence our culture, or is it more important to tell people about Jesus and the spiritual salvation he offers?

DEBATE STARTERS

Can Christians really offer solutions to systematic issues of injustice apart from God changing the hearts of individuals?

Do Christians ultimately "fail" if they help someone rise up out of poverty but that person never becomes a Christian?

Can we really say that evangelism is more important than addressing material needs in light of James 2:14-26?

Is it possible that some Christians will be more effective at evangelism while others are more effective at addressing injustice, or is this a false dichotomy?

—

YES

Addressing issues of injustice is the most important way we can influence our culture.

THOUGHTS

—

NO

It's more important to tell people about Jesus and the spiritual salvation he offers.

THOUGHTS

SEEKING FIRST

REFLECT

Have a few people in the group take turns reading this section aloud.

There is a well-known verse in Jesus' Sermon on the Mount where he talks about kingdom-minded living. He challenges his listeners not to worry about the material things in their lives—what they will eat, drink, or the clothes they will wear. Rather, we should: "Seek first [God's] kingdom and his righteousness, and all these things will be given to you" (Matt. 6:33).

Interestingly, the Greek word that is translated "righteousness" (*dikaiosune*) can also mean "justice." In the Greek language, there is no separate term for "justice"; the concepts of righteousness and justice are intertwined into one word that can be translated either way in English. So, when Jesus challenges us to seek his kingdom first, is he saying that we should seek righteousness—a right standing with God? Or is he saying that we should seek the working out of his justice in the world?

It's probably a combination of both. Which leads us back to the idea that in God's kingdom, justification and justice go hand in hand. In word and deed, we are to be people that embody God's rule in our lives who are utterly dependent on his transformative grace. And we are to embody God's rule in our world by being vessels of his grace and justice toward others who are poor in spirit and physical need.

REFLECTION STARTERS

Spend a few minutes journaling your thoughts to the two questions below. Then, share your reflections with the group.

If people were to examine the way you treat the poor and marginalized, would they conclude that you've fully encountered God's grace in your own life?

What are the most significant reasons that you don't extend God's unconditional grace to the poor and marginalized in your own community? What would it take to change?

JOURNAL

JOURNAL

—

A KINGDOM OF JUSTICE AND MERCY

ACT

—

God's kingdom is a kingdom of justice and mercy. He is a just God who demonstrates mercy toward unjust sinners. In doing so, he transforms unjust sinners into just and merciful agents of his kingdom, that we might become the hands and feet of his justice and mercy in the world.

What is one specific area of justice and mercy that you will engage in this week?

—

THE TRANSFORMATIVE KINGDOM

PREPARE FOR NEXT GATHERING

—

Do an experiment this week: get several one dollar or five dollar bills at the bank, carry them with you, and give one to each person that you see who is begging for money on a street corner. As you do it, take note of your thoughts and emotions. Does this person deserve this free gift? Is it possible this person will abuse this free gift? Use this exercise to reflect on your own relationship with God and be the "mirror" that Tim Keller described.

Spend the final portion of your time together discussing your culture-shaping project.

PLANNING THE CULTURE-SHAPING PROJECT

You'll need to make a decision by the end of this gathering since what you do will likely require planning. Your project needs to take place before your last group gathering and it should be something that everyone can participate in. You can review the suggestions given on pages 94-95. It may be difficult to find total agreement among the group, but try to establish some consensus by talking through the advantages and disadvantages of all suggestions. Don't be afraid to think creatively and challenge yourselves. You're not limited by the suggestions included in this study, but you'll want to undertake something that will help you apply what you've been learning. Make a decision and solidify action steps before you conclude.

For me Christianity is about the Kingdom, not about the Church: it has to do with human growth and development, not church growth and development.

MICHAEL TAYLOR

Our faith is stronger than death, our philosophy is firmer than flesh, and the spread of the Kingdom of God upon the earth is more sublime and more compelling.

DOROTHY DAY

When we quit thinking primarily about ourselves and our own self-preservation, we undergo a truly heroic transformation of consciousness.

JOSEPH CAMPBELL

THE TRANSFORMATIVE KINGDOM

OUR MISSION

DISCUSS

Spend a few minutes sharing your thoughts with the group.

Every organization has a mission statement. But not every organization actually lives by its mission statement. In fact, some of their actions would demonstrate otherwise. People can be the same way too. If someone examined your life, what would they conclude about your mission statement?

DISCUSSION STARTERS

If someone examined your checkbook, credit card bill, and the way you spend your money, what would they conclude about your mission in life?

If someone looked at your schedule, calendar, and the way you spend your time, what would they conclude about your mission in life?

If someone took note of the things you celebrate, what would they conclude about your mission in life?

FAMOUS MISSION STATEMENTS

TO ORGANIZE THE WORLD'S INFORMATION AND MAKE IT UNIVERSALLY ACCESSIBLE AND USEFUL.

GOOGLE

TO PRODUCE INNOVATIVE, POPULAR, AND PROFITABLE ENTERTAINMENT IN THE BEST CREATIVE ENVIRONMENT.

NEW LINE CINEMA

OUR VISION IS TO BE EARTH'S MOST CUSTOMER-CENTRIC COMPANY; TO BUILD A PLACE WHERE PEOPLE CAN COME TO FIND AND DISCOVER ANYTHING THEY MIGHT WANT TO BUY ONLINE.

AMAZON.COM

TO CREATE, PRESERVE, AND DISSEMINATE KNOWLEDGE.

YALE UNIVERSITY

TO PROVIDE RELIEF TO VICTIMS OF DISASTER AND HELP PEOPLE PREVENT, PREPARE FOR, AND RESPOND TO EMERGENCIES.

RED CROSS

—

THE TRANSFORMATIVE KINGDOM

WATCH

—

View Q Talk: The Transformative Kingdom by Jon Tyson.

Record your thoughts on the talk on page 83.

Jon Tyson is a church planter and lead pastor of Trinity Grace Church, located in New York City. He is also on the board of directors of the Origins Movement, a new church planting movement committed to multiplying missional church communities in the major urban centers of the world.

When Jesus ascended into heaven, he left his followers with the mission of sharing his gospel and extending his kingdom movement into the world. How did he do this? What did he share with them before he left? How did he make sure they got the "mission statement"? At Q Chicago, Jon Tyson explained how Jesus transformed his followers after his resurrection and how it prepared them to be agents of his transformative kingdom in the world.

—

"The time between the resurrection of Jesus and the ascension of Jesus and Pentecost is one of the most tender revelations about what matters to the heart of Jesus and his movement."

—

"What is most important to the movement of Jesus? The people near to him who will carry this out."

—

"The Jesus kingdom is better than the kingdom they thought they could establish."

—

"Jesus goes to the greatest failures in the church and he brings them back together and recommissions them based on his goal and his power, not their morality."

THOUGHTS

ARE THE DISCIPLES OUR MODEL?

Split the group into two sides and spend fifteen minutes debating the issue:

Are we supposed to follow the radical examples of the early disciples who became zealous missionaries in their culture?

Even if you don't agree with the side you are representing, consider and offer the best arguments for your position. Be respectful.

Record your thoughts on pages 86-87.

Use the following debate starters to guide your time.

As Jon Tyson explained, Jesus spent focused time with the disciples after the resurrection—restoring them after their failures and transforming them into the "missionaries" they would be for his kingdom mission. And the book of Acts tells us about the many amazing things that happened as thousands saw their changed lives, heard their message, and put their faith in Christ. But aren't our lives and our context so different now? Does God really expect all of us to follow in the footsteps of those early disciples?

Are we supposed to follow the radical examples of the early disciples who became zealous missionaries in their culture?

DEBATE STARTERS

Many of the early disciples traveled around like Paul, preaching and starting churches. Is this the only example of living the kingdom life? Is it the best example? Or is it just one way?

How would you define "missionary"? Does it only describe people who go to foreign lands?

How could you be a missionary of the kingdom in your current channel of culture or neighborhood?

Does reading the accounts of the early church in Acts encourage you or discourage you? Why?

—

YES

We should follow the radical examples of the early disciples and become zealous missionaries in our own culture.

THOUGHTS

NO

The culture and context of the early disciples was very different; we aren't all called to follow their examples.

THOUGHTS

—

AFTER PENTECOST

REFLECT

—

Have a few people in the group take turns reading this section aloud.

It's been said that the disciples went back to fishing after Jesus' resurrection. Only after Pentecost—when they received the Holy Spirit—did the trajectory of their lives radically change. Only then did they truly understand the power and responsibility in being agents of God's kingdom.

It's easy to neglect the role of the Holy Spirit in our lives. He's always in the background, mysterious, intangible, and sometimes, unnoticeable. If we think of him at all, it's usually as a comforter during difficult times. But when it comes to mission-minded kingdom living, the Holy Spirit couldn't be more central. As theologian Bruce Shelley writes, "The Spirit's specific mission is to empower God's liberating forces launched by the appearance of Jesus Christ" (*Theology for Ordinary People*, InterVarsity Press, 1993, p. 118). In other words, the only way Christians can live out God's kingdom, bringing liberation and restoration to our world, is through our dependence on the Holy Spirit. Perhaps this is why Jesus said it was better for him to leave so that the Holy Spirit could come (John 16:7).

REFLECTION STARTERS

Spend a few minutes journaling your thoughts to the two questions below. Then, share your reflections with the group.

What is keeping you from fully following Jesus? If you could have your own "Eastertide experience" with Jesus, what would you ask of him?

In what areas of your life do you desire to follow Christ and live in his kingdom, but you're lacking the power? How might the Holy Spirit give you power?

JOURNAL

JOURNAL

—

TRANSFORMATION

ACT

—

In order to follow Jesus, we must allow him to transform us. We cannot bring transformation to our world until we allow the Holy Spirit to begin its work in our lives first. As we deal with our doubts, guilt, shame, and brokenness, God makes us into agents of his kingdom.

How can you serve and encourage someone else in your community as they seek to live out the kingdom way of life?

CULTURE-SHAPING PROJECT

PREPARE FOR NEXT GATHERING

Your primary assignment is to undertake your culture-shaping project before your next gathering. Be intentional about setting aside time to prepare for and execute your project so that you can discuss it when you next meet. Project options follow on pages 94-95.

CULTURE-SHAPING PROJECT

IDEAS FOR GROUP PROJECT

Your group has been discussing the kingdom way of life. Now you have an opportunity to take what you are learning and do something together. Be sure to plan this group project early and undertake it before your final group gathering. Following are three options you might consider.

Option One: Bringing the Kingdom to a Family

Someone in the group likely has a personal connection to a family with someone who has special needs and could use some help. As a group, decide how each person can use their talents and gifts to come alongside that individual and family to let them experience the fullness of life in the coming weeks. What can you do to serve them? Consider helping with house projects, one-on-one tutoring, or offering childcare so that parents can experience an evening out. Live the gospel to this family.

1

Option Two: Bringing the Kingdom to a Neighborhood

Identify one area of neighborhood life that is "broken" for the families or children that live there. How can your group bring the kingdom to bear physically by addressing that challenge? Make plans for a community garden that can aid an urban population with fresh vegetables. Fix up a dilapidated playground. Pick up trash. Or help an elderly family that has a hard time with taking care of their home during the changing seasons. Live out the gospel in your neighborhood.

Option Three: Bringing the Kingdom to a City

There are many great organizations in your city addressing poverty, homelessness, teenage pregnancy, and other challenging issues. Be generous with your time by scheduling a time when your group can spend a few hours assisting a local nonprofit organization that serves the poor in your city. Habitat for Humanity, food banks, homeless shelters, and crisis pregnancy centers are great options to consider. Ask the organization you contact what their needs are (not if they can accommodate you), then step in and help. Live out the gospel in your city.

People must not only hear about the kingdom of God, but must see it in actual operation, on a small scale perhaps and in imperfect form, but a real demonstration nevertheless.

PANDITA RAMABAI

I will place no value on anything I have or may possess except in relation to the kingdom of Christ.

DAVID LIVINGSTONE

If you have not chosen the Kingdom of God first, it will in the end make no difference what you have chosen instead.

WILLIAM LAW

SEEKING THE HIDDEN TREASURE

—

EVALUATING THE PROJECT

DISCUSS

—

Over the past several weeks, you've been exposed to some new ideas. Your group has discussed and debated how these concepts might change the way you think about faith and culture. And you've worked on a group project together to begin considering how these ideas might change the way you live your lives. Spend some time evaluating what you learned during your group project.

DISCUSSION STARTERS

How difficult was it to undertake your group project?

Did you find any part of it uncomfortable or not helpful? Why?

What's the most important thing you learned during your group project?

What are the biggest barriers for you personally in living out the kingdom way of life?

THOUGHTS

—

THIS IS WHAT IT'S LIKE

—

Have a few people in the group take turns reading this section aloud.

Jesus told many stories about the kingdom of God (or heaven). Listen to several of them:

> Jesus told them another parable: "The kingdom of heaven is like a man who sowed good seed in his field. But while everyone was sleeping, his enemy came and sowed weeds among the wheat, and went away. When the wheat sprouted and formed heads, then the weeds also appeared.
>
> "The owner's servants came to him and said, 'Sir, didn't you sow good seed in your field? Where then did the weeds come from?'
>
> "'An enemy did this,' he replied.
>
> "The servants asked him, 'Do you want us to go and pull them up?'
>
> "'No,' he answered, 'because while you are pulling the weeds, you may uproot the wheat with them. Let both grow together until the harvest. At that time I will tell the harvesters: First collect the weeds and tie them in bundles to be burned;

then gather the wheat and bring it into my barn.'"

--

He told them another parable: "The kingdom of heaven is like a mustard seed, which a man took and planted in his field. Though it is the smallest of all seeds, yet when it grows, it is the largest of garden plants and becomes a tree, so that the birds come and perch in its branches."

--

He told them still another parable: "The kingdom of heaven is like yeast that a woman took and mixed into about sixty pounds of flour until it worked all through the dough."

--

"The kingdom of heaven is like treasure hidden in a field. When a man found it, he hid it again, and then in his joy went and sold all he had and bought that field.

--

"Again, the kingdom of heaven is like a merchant looking for fine pearls. When he found one of great value, he went away and sold everything he had and bought it."
—Matthew 13:24–33, 44–46

REFLECTION STARTERS

Spend a few minutes journaling your thoughts to these questions, then share with the group.

Which of these stories stood out to you most, and why?

What do you learn about the kingdom of God from these stories?

JOURNAL

JOURNAL

LIFE IN THE KINGDOM

ACT

Share your final thoughts with the group about your experience during this study.

How do you view the kingdom way of life differently as a result of this Q study?

What have you learned?

What will you change about your lifestyle in the future?

What will you start doing?

What will you stop doing?

Spend the last fifteen minutes of your gathering praying as a group.

If you've never prayed out loud with other people, don't let this intimidate you. Your prayers need not be elaborate or articulate. Simply talk to God. Use these suggestions to guide your time::

- Pray for God's kingdom rule in your own life.

- Pray for God's kingdom rule in your small group.

- Pray for God's kingdom rule in your neighborhood.

- Pray for God's kingdom rule in your church.

- Pray for God's kingdom rule in your city.

- Pray for God's kingdom rule in the world.

Thy kingdom come, thy will be done, on earth as it is in heaven.

Share Your Thoughts

With the Author: Your comments will be forwarded to the author when you send them to *zauthor@zondervan.com*.

With Zondervan: Submit your review of this book by writing to *zreview@zondervan.com*.

Free Online Resources at

www.zondervan.com

Zondervan AuthorTracker: Be notified whenever your favorite authors publish new books, go on tour, or post an update about what's happening in their lives at www.zondervan.com/authortracker.

Daily Bible Verses and Devotions: Enrich your life with daily Bible verses or devotions that help you start every morning focused on God. Visit www.zondervan.com/newsletters.

Free Email Publications: Sign up for newsletters on Christian living, academic resources, church ministry, fiction, children's resources, and more. Visit www.zondervan.com/newsletters.

Zondervan Bible Search: Find and compare Bible passages in a variety of translations at www.zondervanbiblesearch.com.

Other Benefits: Register yourself to receive online benefits like coupons and special offers, or to participate in research.

ZONDERVAN.com/
AUTHOR**TRACKER**
follow your favorite authors